# BRIDGING THE WORLD

Xiu Yi Bridge, Beijing

# BRIDGING THE WORLD

Robert S. Cortright

BRIDGE INK
32580 SW Arbor Lake Drive
Wilsonville, Oregon 97070

Library of Congress Control Number: 2003094276

ISBN: 0-9641963-3-6

BRIDGE INK
32580 SW Arbor Lake Drive
Wilsonville, Oregon  97070

Editing, Jeanne Cortright Neff
Binding, Lincoln & Allen
Printed in USA by Millcross Litho

Dedicated to the memory of my late wife, Kathy

For her support and encouragement in spite
of having to wait patiently at every bridge.

Liberty Bridge, Budapest

# CONTENTS

# BRIDGING THE WORLD

*ridging the World* is the third in a series of pictorial books designed to share a passion for and appreciation of the beauty of bridges. The first volume, published in 1994, was *"Bridging,"* a selection of bridges in America and Europe. Next, in 1998 was *"Bridging, Discovering the Beauty of Bridges,"* a more comprehensive presentation intended to heighten awareness of the aesthetics of bridges.

Each of the previous books brought contact with a number of readers from near and far. It has been especially gratifying to learn that many who weren't previously conscious of bridges now see and admire the bridges around them. They have discovered the beauty of bridges.

Those contacts have been expanded through an internet website featuring a *Bridge of the Month Quiz* which invites viewers to join in the fun of identifying a new bridge picture each month at www.bridgeink.com .

To provide material to justify the title of this book, *"Bridging the World,"* I have continued travelling to photograph interesting bridges until the new volume could include examples from all of the world's populated continents. I hope you enjoy the results.

# BRIDGE TYPES

## Beam Bridges

The most basic type of bridge is the beam. A beam bridge can be as simple as a tree trunk across a small stream or as complicated as the mighty cantilever span at the Firth of Forth in Scotland. The type includes simple stone and concrete slabs, all types of wood or metal trusses and girders of concrete or steel. The unifying feature is that the beam has the necessary rigidity to bear a load between its supports.

Scotland's Forth Railroad Bridge was the longest span bridge in the world when it was completed in 1890. Its giant cantilevers provide two open spans of 1,710 feet each. Its massive tubular frame is said to be a conscious reaction to the public concern about bridge safety after a recent disaster in the nearby Firth of Tay.

The Taiping Bridge at Tongli Town in China's Jiangsu Province is a much simpler beam bridge. Its ornate stone slabs span only 14 feet.

The Ölandsbron stretches 6 kilometers to connect the island of Öland to the mainland of Sweden. Its multiple concrete beams have a maximum span of 472 feet.

Though one of the least appealing of the many bridges at Mérida, Spain, this railroad span is a good example of a truss--another form of the beam.

Though much more sophisticated than a tree trunk across a stream, the Ponte degli Alpini in Bassano, Italy is just another form of wooden beam. The design originated in the 16th century with the famous architect Andrea Palladio. Over the years the bridge has been rebuilt many times, faithfully adhering to his distinctive plan. The most recent reconstruction was in 1966.

The variety of styles of the beam bridge is seemingly endless, but most examples are not likely candidates for a book devoted to the presentation of bridge aesthetics.

Continuous steel truss, Oregon

Wooden through truss, Canada

Lattice truss, Scotland

Steel through truss, Arizona

Temporary "Bailey" bridge, Italy

Steel deck truss, Oregon

Wooden beams, Tasmania

There are many exceptions to the assumption that beam bridges lack aesthetic appeal. Certainly one of those exceptions is the starkly handsome Clermont Ferrand Viaduct. Technically, this bridge is a concrete box girder with inclined piers. Completed in 1992, it carries the modern motorway over the Truyére River near St. Flour in the south of France. It shares that spectacular site with Gustave Eiffel's nearby Garabit Viaduct. (See page 85.)

The Gouritz River Highway Bridge is another striking example of a concrete box girder supported on inclined piers. The 557 foot span was built in 1977. Located on South Africa's Garden Route, it is one of three parallel bridges soaring above the gorge of the Gouritz River. It replaced the old steel cantilever highway bridge built in 1892. That structure is now the popular launching site for bungy jumping. (I resisted the temptation.) Other Garden Route bridges are featured on pages 106 and 111.

The Douro River at Porto, Portugal is spanned by four fascinating bridges from the 19th and 20th centuries. The Ponte Sâo Joâo (above ) is the newest of these, built in 1991. The cantilever of reinforced concrete was designed by the city's famous engineer, Edgar Cardoso. The main span is 820 feet. Cardoso's other bridge at Porto is the Arrábida Bridge, a concrete arch pictured on page 110. The oldest of the Porto bridges is Eiffel's Ponte Maria Pia, partially visible in the background and also pictured on page 84.

Beam bridges are the most common of forms as they include the mundane, the ordinary and the uninteresting. Therefore, they are underrepresented in a collection devoted to the beauty of bridges.

More impressive than beautiful is the storied Pont Quebec. The first attempt to construct a cantilever here ended in disaster in 1907 when the partially completed bridge collapsed into the St. Lawrence River taking the lives of 75 workmen and ruining the reputation of bridge engineer Theodore Cooper. Another mishap on the newly designed second attempt cost 11 fatalities before the span was completed in 1917. The cantilever span measures 1,800 feet, still the longest in the world.

The Ponte Internationale at Valenca do Minho, Portugal is not beautiful, but not ordinary either. It carries rail traffic atop and auto traffic within its wrought iron lattice girder. It was built in 1885 by Gustave Eiffel. Eiffel was a leading bridge builder before he gained fame for construction of the Eiffel Tower in Paris.

# BRIDGE TYPES

## Arch Bridges

he arch bridge is often attributed to the ancient Romans, but the arch was actually in use for many centuries before their time. The fact that many Roman bridges and aqueducts are still viable today attests to the strength of the arch as well as to the skill of the builders.

In addition to its inherent strength, the arch has undeniable aesthetic appeal. It is employed in a wide variety of forms and materials, from the ancient to the most modern.

The essence of this series of books is the appreciation of the beauty of bridges. With that in mind, a dominant portion of this book is devoted to a worldwide sampling of bridges of the arch form. The arch bridge section of this book is further divided by the material employed; first the masonry arch bridges.

The Pont St. Martin in northern Italy's Aosta valley has a span of 120 feet, the longest of any surviving Roman bridge. Experts disagree as to the age of the bridge. Estimates of its origin range from 140 B.C. to 25 B.C.

13

The arch bridges in these pages are arranged in roughly chronological order. "Roughly" because many of the old bridges are dated with considerable uncertainty.

The Ponte dell'Abadia on the opposite page is possibly the oldest presented here. Built at the site of the ancient Roman town of Vulci north of Rome, the existing Roman bridge is believed to date from 90 B.C. The foundations of the bridge are thought to be Etruscan which would give the bridge claim to pre-Roman origins.

The oldest bridge in the center of Rome is this remnant which is now known as the Ponte "Rotto" (broken bridge). Originally known as Pons Aemilius, it was built in 179 B.C. The only portion remaining is this ornate arch in the center of the Tiber River.

The Ponte S. Angelo is the most elaborate of the spans which have survived since Roman times in the city of Rome. Built in 134 A.D. in the time of Emperor Hadrian, it connects the Castel Sant' Angelo with the area of the Vatican.

It has undergone a number of alterations and renovations over the centuries, but has retained its basic original form.

The statuary adorning the bridge dates from the 16th and 17th centuries. The most recent of these are the eight angels attributed to Bernini and his students.

Construction of this bridge in Rimini, Italy was commenced during the reign of Augustus and completed in 20 A.D. during the reign of Emperor Tiberius. Though it is often referred to as Ponte Augusto, I use the name Ponte de Tiberio because that's what the signs say which direct a heavy flow of modern traffic over the bridge.

Considered by many to be the most beautiful of the Roman bridges, it was admired and copied in the 16th century by the famous architect, Andrea Palladio.

The Romans were famous for the network of roads that they built to the far ends of their empire. These projects necessarily included numerous bridges. Many of the finest remaining examples of Roman bridge building are located beyond what is now Italy.

Perhaps the most impressive is the Alcántara Bridge over the Tagus river in Spain. Caius Julius Lacer completed this bridge in 104 A.D. during the reign of Emperor Trajan. It is one of the few Roman bridges whose builder is credited with its construction. Lacer's words appear on an inscription at the site, *"I have built a bridge which will remain for ever."* So far, so good!

Nowhere is the power and beauty of the Roman arch better illustrated than in the massive vaults of the Puente Romano in Mérida, Spain. This bridge was built around 25 B.C. The longest of the remaining Roman bridges, it reaches over 2,000 feet across the Guadiana River.

After the fall of the Roman Empire, there was a period of decline in the western world during which there was evidently no progress in bridge building. In China, however, there remain examples of arched stone bridges built as long ago as the 7th century exhibiting a level of sophistication unmatched in the west for hundreds of years.

The largest and most famous of these is the Zhazhou Bridge (also known as the Anji Bridge) in Hebei province. It is said to date from the year 605 and its span is 121 feet. Its segmental arch (a flattened arch which is only a small part of a circle) and its open spandrels (the openings between the roadway and the main arch) are in sharp contrast to the semicircular arches and solid spandrels common in Roman bridges.

The Zhazhou Bridge is carefully restored and proudly displayed as the centerpiece in a public park setting. I heartily approve of those efforts, but there are a number of old bridges in China of the same style as Zhazhou and I found some of the smaller and less pampered spans to be even more charming.

At Dongqiao village, the beautiful Hongji Bridge is the center of activity. Its structure is very similar to the Zhazhou Bridge and it probably dates from the same era.

During my visit, the Fangshun Bridge was the center of a local gathering. Its typical side arches are now mostly buried in the earth as is a portion of the main arch.

The Yongtong Bridge (below) was guarded by ferocious stone lions.

Both spans were difficult to date, but were similar in structure to the Zhazhou Bridge.

While most bridges are built for primarily for utilitarian purposes, many of the old bridges in China were built for beauty alone.

One of the oldest of these is the Jingxing Qialoudian Bridge which arches over a precipitous cleft in the rock supporting this temple in China's scenic Cangyan Mountains. The bridge is said to have been built in the years 581 to 600.

Reaching this site required a climb up 300 steep stone steps. To get into position to take this picture, I accepted my guide's generous offer to let me stand on his shoulders.

The Baodai Bridge in the suburbs of Suzhou City, Jiangsu Province of China, was completed in the year 819. Fifty-three arches make up its length of over 1,000 feet.

In spite of the murky weather that persisted during my visit, this impressive old relic was a delightful sight.

Throughout most of Europe, during the "dark ages" after the fall of Rome, no important strides were made in bridge building. An exception was the activity of the Moors. From 711 to 1492 the Moors ruled a major part of Spain, and the peninsula enjoyed a period of economic and cultural growth which included instances of maintaining or rebuilding Roman bridges. The Puente Alcántara in Toledo was built by the Moors on the site of a former Roman bridge. It was reconstructed again in the 13th century after being destroyed in a flood. Its main arch over the Tagus River has a span of 93 feet.

Much the same is true of the Puente Romano in Córdoba, Spain. The original structure is believed to date from the 1st century when Córdoba was an important Roman town. The Moors occupied Córdoba in the 8th century and it flourished as one of the most brilliant cities in Europe. During that period the bridge was reconstructed and it still serves Córdoba, carrying modern vehicular traffic over its 900-foot length.

In Europe, the art of bridge building was gradually reawakened in the early years of the second millennium. Outstanding examples of masonry arch bridges from the 12th and 13th centuries are preserved and in many cases are still in use.

The Pont d'Avignon was completed in 1188. Its legendary builder was eventually canonized as St. Bénezet. The multiple arches stretched across the Rhone River at Avignon in southern France. Only four of the original 20 or 21 spans remain intact, but the bridge has retained both its fame and its beauty.

The Pont du Diable at the village of Olargues in southern France is said to date from the twelfth century. The same source described this span as a footbridge, but it is actually being used by automobile traffic. Regardless of the accuracy of the information, the gorgeous site begs to be included here.

In Languedoc France, at what is now the city of Béziers, the Roman road Via Domitia crossed the river Orb near this spot. This bridge, the Pont Vieux is often called the Roman Bridge, but it was erected sometime in the 13th or 14th century. As is the case with many medieval bridges, there seems to be no certainty as to its exact age. There is little doubt of its beauty.

The Romans left Britain in 410 A.D. There are many artifacts attesting to their occupation, but contrary to common belief, the British Isles has no bridges remaining from that period. One of the oldest of the surviving medieval bridges is Old Elvet Bridge over the river Wear in Durham, England. Construction was commenced in 1160 by Bishop Pudsey. The bridge has been widened and repaired over the years enabling it to carry modern traffic.

1272 is the commonly accepted date for the construction of the Monnow Bridge over the Monnow at Monmouth in Wales.  This is Britain's best example of a fortified bridge.  The massive structure over the pier once contained a portcullis, a heavy defensive gate which could be moved up and down in grooves within the stone walls of the tower to control access to the town.

The Pont sur la Bévéra has served the town of Sospel, near Nice in southern France since the 12th century. Over the years it has been rebuilt at various times. Most recently it was fully restored in 1953 after sustaining damage during World War II. One of the interesting challenges in "bridging" is to find the ideal vantage point from which to photograph the subject. I have a fond memory of being graciously escorted upstairs to a second floor flat. Planters of geraniums were shoved aside to clear the way to a small balcony commanding this view of the bridge.

The Pont des Trous in Tournai, Belgium was built in 1281, 1290 or 1329, take your pick. Behind those flags on the protected bridge deck is a fine place to sit under an umbrella and have a glass of excellent Belgian beer. "Bridging" is not all hard work.

From the diary of Marco Polo, *"Over this river there is a very fine stone bridge, so fine indeed, that it has very few equals in the world."* When this entry was written in 1280, The Lugou Bridge near Beijing, China was already almost 100 years old. It is remembered not only as the "Marco Polo Bridge" but also as the site of the commencement of hostilities with Japan in 1937.

Its eleven arches which stretch 700 feet across the Yongding River are adorned by 485 stone lions.

The Ponte Fortficada de Ucanha lays claim to being the only remaining fortified bridge in Portugal. One description states that in 1146 it was already mentioned as "old." Another reference mentions Roman origins but, the acknowledged experts do not include it in their lists of Roman bridges. In any case, the bridge at the village of Ucanha, near the town of Tarouca, is an imposing structure. The entrance to the bridge is protected by a two-story tower which has in times past served as a toll collection station as well as a fortification at the river crossing.

The lovely village of Lagrasse was briefly our base of operations for "bridging" in the Languedoc region of France.

The Pont Vieux, built in 1308, was reason enough for a visit, but the charm of the town surpassed the beauty of the bridge.

(The Pont Neuf in the foreground is about 500 years newer.)

The south of France, having escaped much of the devastation of 20th century wars, boasts many fine bridges which have survived since medieval times.

At Villefranche, on the banks of the Aveyron, the Consuls bridge of 1321 was once topped by two watchtowers.

The Pont Vieux over the Lot River in Espalion is variously described as of 12th, 13th or 14th century origin. One old book insists that its construction was ordered by Charlemagne between 768 and 814. The same text describes it as "*a barbaric work without any interest at all as architecture.*"

According to legend, the Countess Matilda of Tuscany had the Ponte della Maddalena built in 1101 to enable her to cross the river Serchio to visit health-giving springs. The bridge near Bagni di Lucca, Italy was constructed in its present form in 1317. It is also known as Ponte del Diavolo--Devil's Bridge, one of many bridges worldwide sharing a devil's legend.

The most famous of Italy's medieval bridges is the Ponte Vecchio. Built in 1345 by Taddeo Gaddi, it was the only bridge over the Arno in Florence which was spared when the German army retreated in 1944. The Ponte Vecchio is one of the few remaining examples of the medieval practice of erecting buildings on the bridge deck. The bridge's shops were initially occupied by various tradesmen, but since 1593 by gold- and silversmiths.

One of the oldest surviving bridges in Germany is in such good condition that it appears to be one of the newest. The Old Lahn Bridge at Limburg was built in 1315. The target of allied bombers in 1944, it was repaired in 1948 and further renovated in 1983. For many years tolls extracted for passage over the Lahn River provided a major part of Limburg's income.

The Charles Bridge in Prague was instrumental in my early appreciation of bridges. It was built over an extended period in the 14th century, probably completed in 1380. Its sixteen arches are adorned by many elaborate statues including that of St. John of Nepomuk. Legend has it that Nepomuk was thrown from the Charles Bridge to his death for refusing to reveal the secrets of the Queen's confessional.

He is considered the saint of rivers and rivermen and his statues adorn a number of bridges throughout Europe. In fact, the figure on the railing of the Old Lahn Bridge on the preceding page is a statue of St. Nepomuk.

Pont Valentré, the symbol of the city of Cahors, was the primary target of a recent bridging expedition to the south of France.

This masterpiece is perhaps the most magnificent and best preserved medieval fortified bridge in the world. Construction was commenced in 1308 and not completed until some 70 years later.

It has six arches and three impressive square towers which soar 130 feet above the River Lot. Only by scrambling up the cliff on the left was I able to squeeze all three towers into a photograph.

The Pont Vieux at Montauban, France was completed in 1335. Its seven red brick arches stretch 672 feet across the River Tarn. The openings over the piers serve a dual purpose of reducing the weight on the foundations and allowing more water to flow when the river is in flood.

Like its contemporary, the Pont Valentré at Cahors, the original configuration included square protective towers at each end. The tower at one end, where the executioner lived, was removed in 1663. The other was replaced by a triumphal arch in 1701. The bridge has been widened as recently as 1881 and, as is evident in this picture, it still carries a heavy load of modern traffic.

The bridge over the Aveyron River at Belcastel, France is said to have been built in the late 14th century. Its pointed or ogival arches are characteristic of medieval bridges constructed in that period. Note that the arches are constructed of large, carefully cut stones while the upper portions are composed of smaller rough material.

Uzbekistan abounds with remarkable architectural treasures which are prime tourist attractions, but it is not a likely place to look for bridges. But at the Zerafshan River on the outskirts of Samarkand, there is a remnant of a seven-arch bridge that dates from the early 14th century. My bridging guide, a waiter from the hotel in Samarkand, is perched on the ogival brick arch. (An ogival arch, common in Islamic architecture, is pointed at the center rather than round.)

This is probably a good place to demonstrate that the load bearing ability of a masonry arch bridge is wholly dependent on the strength of the arch form.

The Zerafshan Arch on the preceding page, the Bridge of Carr in Scotland (right) and the remnants Pont St. Thibéry in France attest to this fact. The Scottish bridge is not quite 300 years old. The Roman bridge at St. Thibéry is almost 2,000.

The name Devil's Bridge and the accompanying story is attached to a number of spans in Britain and beyond. The legend, with local variations, describes a woman who makes a pact with the Devil to build a bridge to enable her to get her cows across the swollen river. In trade, the Devil is granted claim to the first soul to cross the bridge. The woman contrives to get her dog to be the first to cross, and the Devil has to be satisfied with an animal soul.

A bridge friend in England has assured me that the most beautiful of his homeland's many old stone bridges is the Devil's Bridge at Kirkby Lonsdale. I believe him, if not the legend.

Another devil's legend attaches to the medieval Ponte Misarela in Portugal.

A fugitive fleeing from the authorities found himself trapped at the edge of this mountain torrent. The devil offered to provide a bridge in trade for his soul. The deal was made and the devil destroyed the bridge after the man's escape.

Repentant, the man sought the assistance of his priest to regain his soul. He again dealt with the devil for a bridge across the chasm, but this time the wily priest was concealed nearby so as to bless the bridge before the devil could destroy it, thereby preserving the span for all time.

Near the Sicilian town of Adrano there remains a multi-arch stone bridge which dates from the 14th century. The Ponte dei Saraceni spans the turbulent Simento river in a rugged and scenic rural location near Mount Etna.

The name refers to the Saracens who ruled Sicily during the 9th, 10th and 11th centuries.

The old bridge is still in use by pedestrians and judging from the hoof prints on the muddy approach ramps, by cattle.

Another Sicilian bridge is the ornate Ponte San Leonardo at Termini Imerese. It was designed in 1625 by Archbishop Agatino Daidone.

The configuration is unusual in that one of the approach ramps is perpendicular to the main span. According to historians, that end of the bridge rests on the remnants of an ancient bridge from Roman times.

The bridge is no longer in use and the San Leonardo River no longer flows under its graceful arch.

Many of the world's beautiful old bridges are a challenge to photograph because they are situated in crowded urban settings or are screened by nearby foliage. In contrast, at Quézac in southern France, the Pont sur la Tarn spans a peaceful stretch of the river Tarn, just before it drops into the turbulent Gorges du Tarn. No more idyllic site could be found. The bridge was completed in 1450 and still carries modern vehicular traffic.

Scotland's Old Stirling Bridge was built of sandstone in about 1400, replacing a previous wooden span made famous by its critical role in the Battle of Stirling in 1297. Those readers who have copies of my earlier publication, *Bridging, Discovering the Beauty of Bridges,* might recall another view of this charming stone arch bridge from the cover of that book.

Mostar in Bosnia was named for the beautiful Stari Most (Old Bridge) which soared over the Neretva River. Constructed by the Ottoman Turks in 1566, for four centuries it was the cherished centerpiece of the city. In 1993 it was destroyed, a victim of civil war in the former Yugoslavia. This photo was taken in happier times when tourists who flocked to the bridge were entertained by daredevil divers. International efforts are now underway to reconstruct the bridge.

No collection of beautiful bridges is complete without Venice's most renowned Rialto Bridge. Completed in 1592 it was designed by Antonio da Ponte. Tradition has it that his design was selected in preference to plans proposed by, among others, Michelangelo and Palladio. It is said that the thrust of the stone arch is borne by 12,000 wooden piles driven into the soft ground on the sides of the Grand Canal.

The Pont Neuf in Paris was completed in 1606. It is the oldest of that city's remaining bridges across the Seine. The picture at left shows how old it appeared in my 1998 book. Since then, it has been returned to splendor in an effective job of clean-up.

As Pont Neuf simply means "New Bridge," the name is not at all unique. One of the most impressive is the Pont Neuf in Toulouse, France. Construction was started in 1544 but not completed until 1632. The unusual openings in the spandrel walls serve to reduce the dead weight on the foundations and also allow increased water flow during flood conditions. The feature undoubtedly contributed to the survival of the bridge when the Garonne River reached the tops of the arches in 1875.

The Kantara Moulay Ismael in Khenifra, Morocco dates from about 1700. In its original form is was hump-backed as depicted in the inset. The present level roadway is obviously a more modern accommodation for wheeled vehicles. The red tones in the buildings, the water and the bridge itself are typical of Khenifra. The garbage strewn on the river banks is regrettably typical of many bridge sites worldwide.

Sultan Moulay Ismael
ruled Morocco from 1672
to 1727.  Massive building
projects were completed
during his reign, including
the bridges on these  two
pages.

The ten-arch Kantara
Ismaelia is at Kasba Tadla,
one of the Sultan's outposts
on the Tadla plain between
Fes and Marrakech.

One of the great delights in "bridging" is the discovery of an unexpected gem. On the road from Meknes to Fes in Morocco we came upon this now bypassed road bridge across the Oued Najat. The graceful five-arch span would be lovely without its elaborate decorations. With them it is stunning.

Masonry Arch Bridges

Beijing's Summer Palace is a treasure trove of purely ornamental Qing Dynasty (1736 - 1795) spans which represent the ultimate in bridge aesthetics. The most famous, at left and opposite, is the Yudai or Jade Belt Bridge with its towering humped arch. Across the lake is the Shiqikong Bridge, its railing adorned with lions. "Shiqikong" means Seventeen Arch.

China's canal bridges take many forms but the masonry arch is predominate. The arch of the Liija Bridge at Changshu City, Jiangsu Provence forms a perfect circle with its reflection in the canal.

The Wumen Bridge crosses the busy Grand Canal in the city of Suzhou. It was originally built in the Song Dynasty (960 - 1278) and rebuilt in 1872.

The extensive Qing Dynasty Tombs in Hebei Province, China have a profusion of ornamental marble bridges, large and small.

The single-arch Yi Kong Qiao at Yu Fei Tomb is typical with an arch span of only about 7 feet.

The five-arch Wu Kong Qiao on the Holy Road is one of the largest.

The figure in the distance is not the usual lion, but a huge marble elephant!

Alte Brücke, Heidelberg, Germany

There are enough interesting masonry arch bridges extant from the 18th century to fill another book. Famous structures in Heidelberg, Germany and Ronda, Spain appear regularly in bridge books. But there are also many little known spans too charming to leave out.

Each of the opposite bridges has special appeal. Skala du Port in Essaouira, Morocco has a unique fortress setting. The Tullbron at Falkenberg is one of Sweden's oldest bridges. The Lion Bridge at Alnwick, England shows off its castellations and its handsome lion.

Puente Nuevo,
Ronda, Spain

Skala du Port, Essaouira, Morocco

Tullbron, Falkenberg, Sweden

Lion Bridge, Alnwick, England

and the Lion

These last two selections of 18th century bridges were chosen on the basis of "degree of difficulty."

The dilemma at Inverary, Scotland was that the Aray Bridge carries the highway on the very edge of Loch Fyne, making it impossible to attain a broadside view. The solution was to drive to the local fishing port, hire the "Gypsy King" and boat to the desired vantage point.

The attractive bridge was designed by Robert Mylne and built in 1776.

Locating the Ponte Alfano was the difficulty in Sicily. My research had turned up a hint of a bridge named Ponte Saraceno di Noto. Armed with that information and a small picture of the bridge, I searched for the better part of a day following false leads in the area surrounding the city of Noto. Finally, the very helpful staff of the local tourist office spent an hour on the phone and found the bridge at nearby Canicattini Bagni under the name Ponte Alfano.

Legend has it that the statues on the portal represent two rival guards who fought to the death on the bridge.

The oldest bridge in Australia is the Richmond Bridge over the Coal River at Richmond on the island of Tasmania. The plaque at midstream reads "A.D 1823." Historical records reflect that the construction was commenced in 1823 and completed in 1825.

The Ross Bridge over the Macquarie River at Ross, Tasmania was completed by convict labor in 1836. The two skilled masons responsible for the ornate stonework were granted emancipation at the completion of the project.

Arch bridges of stone are not frequently encountered in America, but the Starrucca Viaduct at Lanesboro, Pennsylvania is an outstanding exception. Its 17 arches of blue stone carry the railroad 1,040 feet across the valley of Starrucca Creek. It was completed in 1848 and still carries modern rail traffic.

The photographer's model provides some idea of the massive scale of the 100-foot-high arches.

In the second half of the 19th century, conditions were favorable for the construction of numerous stone bridges in Napa Valley, California. Immigrant artisans familiar with stone masonry, a ready supply of good local stone and ample cheap labor contributed to the concentration of some fine arch spans. The most dramatic of these is the Pope Street Bridge at St. Helena. The three-arch bridge was built in 1894 and has a main span of 50 feet.

# BRIDGE TYPES

## Metal Arch Bridges

he arch bridges illustrated to this point have all been constructed of masonry (stone or brick) in the form that takes best advantage of the compressive strength of those materials. That form is the "deck arch" wherein the roadway rests on top of supporting arch or arches. With the advent of modern materials which have strength in tension as well as in compression, new forms of the arch have been employed.

The three basic forms
of arch bridges are:

The deck arch.

Salt River Canyon,
Arizona

The through arch.

Davenport,
Iowa

The half-through arch.

Stockholm,
Sweden

Iron was employed in ancient times to clamp blocks of stone together in bridges. But metal was not employed as a main structural element until Abraham Darby's innovative arch was built in 1779. At Coalbrookdale, Darby constructed his cast-iron arch bridge across England's Severn River. The world's first iron bridge still carries foot traffic and is a major tourist attraction in the town which is now called Ironbridge.

Departing from the organization of the previous section, the selected arch bridges of iron and steel which follow are introduced in order of length of span. The Ironbridge on the previous page is the first exception. Its span is 100 feet while the Pont des Arts presented here has multiple arches spanning just 60 feet each. This lovely pedestrian bridge across the Seine in Paris was first built in iron in 1803. The current version, rebuilt of modern steel, but faithful to the original design, was completed in 1985. Apropos of the bridge's name, the crowds of people shown here are admiring a sculpture exhibit.

There were many interesting iron arch bridges constructed in the early 19th century. The Wye Bridge at Chepstow, Wales was built in 1816 with a maximum span of 112 feet.

Thomas Telford designed a variety of important bridges of many types. At Craigellachie, Scotland he ornamented this graceful cast-iron arch with castellated stone towers. The 150-foot span was built in 1814.

Central Oregon's Crooked River Gorge provides a spectacular setting for a trio of deck arch bridges. The two steel arches were designed by prominent engineers.

In the foreground, the Oregon Trunk Railroad Bridge, built in 1911, was the work of Ralph Modjeski. The span is 325 feet.

Conde B. McCullough was the designer of the Crooked River highway bridge in 1926. Its 330-foot span soars 295 feet above the Crooked River.

The third, a red concrete arch, completed in 2000, is barely visible behind the McCullough bridge.

Completed in 1874, the Eads Bridge at St. Louis was a giant step forward in the development of steel arch bridges. It was conceived by James B. Eads, a man who had never built a bridge. The three tubular arches span the Mississippi in leaps 502, 520 and 502 feet. Here it still stands firm in the spring floods of the mighty river.

There is no better place in the world to view the iron arches of the 19th century than Porto, Portugal. Gustave Eiffel, the same engineer who created the Eiffel tower, was the designer of the Ponte Maria Pia. Built in 1877, this 525-foot iron arch span carried rail traffic over the Douro River for 114 years.

Theophile Seyrig, an associate of Eiffel, was the designer of the Ponte Luiz I, an unusual combination of deck arch and through arch that carries traffic over Porto's Douro River on two levels. The 566-foot span was completed in 1885 and is still carrying heavy traffic on both decks.

Gustave Eiffel's most famous bridge, the Garabit Viaduct, is a slightly longer version of the Ponte Maria Pia. This spectacular 541-foot iron arch has carried rail traffic though France's Massif Central since 1885. The deck was originally 400 feet above the Truyère River, but the water level has been raised considerably since the construction of the Grandval Dam in 1960.

These two Danish bridges were designed by Anker Engelund. The Dronning Alexandrines Bro was completed in 1943. The concrete approach arches and 418-foot steel main span give an appearance very reminiscent of the Yaquina Bay Bridge (opposite).

The 3-kilometer-long Storstrømsbroen would not be chosen for a book devoted to beautiful bridges except for the story that attaches to it. On the occasion of the opening of the bridge in 1935, a noted architect made a very critical speech about the looks of the bridge. Anker Engelund's classic reply was, "Yes, maybe the bridge is ugly, but it is so long that the ugliness per meter is very small."

The highway along the Oregon's Pacific coast was completed in 1936 when a series of monumental bridges designed by Conde B. McCullough were inaugurated. The Yaquina Bay Bridge at Newport is a combination of concrete and steel approach arches leading to a steel central span of 600 feet. The ornate concrete pylons are typical of McCullough's style.

The canyons in the western United States have provided ample opportunities for highway engineers to employ the steel deck arch form. With eye-catching results!

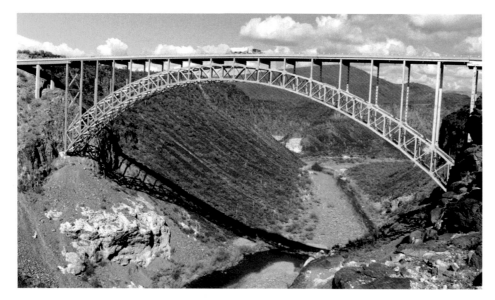

Burro Creek Bridge
Arizona
1965
680-foot span

Cold Springs Canyon
California
1963
700-foot span

Navajo Bridges
Arizona
(L) 834-foot span, 1929
(R) 909-foot span, 1995

Perrine Bridge
Idaho
1976
1140-foot span

The Roosevelt Lake Bridge sits among lakes and mountains in a recreational area in Arizona. It was built in 1990 and has a span of 1079 feet, but carries only a two-lane roadway.

Sharing the same configuration but certainly not the same scale or setting, the Fremont Bridge towers over the Willamette River harbor in the heart of the city of Portland, Oregon. Its 1255-foot main span carries eight traffic lanes on two decks. It was completed in 1973.

There are only two American arch bridges which exceed the Fremont's length of span. Each held the title of world's-longest arch when built.

The Bayonne Bridge which connects New Jersey with Staten Island, New York was completed in 1931 with a span of 1675 feet. Its famous engineer Othmar Ammann was responsible for six of the major spans in the New York City area.

The New River Gorge Bridge in West Virginia took the title in 1977 with a span of 1700 feet. It soars some 876 feet above the water's surface.

The Lupu Bridge, an 1800-foot steel arch in Shanghai, will take over first place in 2003.

It is strikingly similar in design to New York's Hell Gate Bridge which was built in 1917.

The adventurous bridge lover can enjoy the thrill of a "Bridge Climb" atop the giant arch for an unforgettable view of Sydney Harbour and its famous Opera House.

The Sydney Harbour Bridge (opposite) never held the record for long-span arch bridges, but none of its competitors come close to its massive overall dimensions or to its magnificence in its setting. The Australian masterpiece was completed in 1932 and has a span of 1650 feet, just 25 feet less than the Bayonne Bridge.

The massive scale of the bridge is evident in this close-up view of an abutment.

# BRIDGE TYPES

## Concrete Arch Bridges

oncrete was employed as a building material by the Romans, but it didn't come into structural use again until the 18th century. At that time, concrete was used in bridges as a substitute for masonry in forms that took advantage only of its strength in compression. With the advent of the various techniques of reinforcing concrete, bridge designers were able to develop entirely new bridge forms which fully utilize the material's qualities. Included here are examples exhibiting the evolution in style and magnitude of the concrete arch.

Scotland's Glenfinnan Viaduct dates from 1898. It is constructed of mass concrete, that is, without iron or steel reinforcement.

The 90-foot-high arches are the same form used for centuries in stone and brick.

The Alvord Lake Bridge in San Francisco's Golden Gate Park is included entirely for its historic significance. Built in 1888, it is the first reinforced concrete bridge built in the United States. The face of the bridge is hammered concrete imitating stonework. The interior simulates a cave with stalactites and stalagmites in keeping with its connection to a children's playground. The span is only about 20 feet.

In 1911, John B. Leonard designed the reinforced concrete Fernbridge to cross the 2,400-foot bed of the Eel River near Ferndale in northern California. Raging floods have destroyed most of the more modern Eel River bridges over the years, but the 200-foot spans of the Fernbridge stand firm.

In the United States, a wonderful assortment of concrete arch bridges survives from the decade of 1910 to 1920. Rural and urban, large and small, the following examples all enhance their varied settings.

The footbridge at the spectacular Multnomah Falls in Oregon's Columbia River Gorge.

The attractive Rainbow Arch at Folsom, California.

J. A. L. Waddell's ornate Colorado Street Bridge in Pasadena, California.

At almost 1500 feet, this is still the third longest concrete arch bridge in California. It has been the object of restoration efforts to prolong its useful life well into the 21st century.

Main Street Bridge over the Buffalo Bayou in downtown Houston, Texas.

In spite of its advanced age, this graceful arch fits comfortably with the city's modern skyline.

In the 1920s and 1930s, Conde B. McCullough was the state bridge engineer in Oregon at a time when highway infrastructure was rapidly expanding. Two of McCullough's steel arch bridges appear on pages 82 and 87, but his most distinctive style is evidenced in his elegant concrete arch bridges.

The Alsea Bay Bridge at Waldport, Oregon was McCullough's largest concrete structure, reaching a total of 3,011 feet across the mouth of the Alsea River. When completed in 1936, it was widely regarded as one of the finest concrete bridges in America. Unfortunately, it suffered serious structural deterioration as a result of corrosion of its steel reinforcement. It was demolished in 1991.

His biographer credits 50 major spans in Oregon to McCullough. It is no wonder that the state is considered to have one of the world's finest concentrations of concrete arch bridges. Here are a few.

1920 Mosier Creek

1920 Rock Point

1921 Dry Canyon Creek

1922 Myrtle Creek

1924 Winchester

1927 Ben Jones

1931 Caveman

1932 Cape Creek

1932 Gold Beach

The tied arch form of concrete bridge gained popularity in the first half of the 20th century. The Dee Bridge at Kirkudbright, Scotland is a multi-span through tied arch bridge.

Like the Dee Bridge this small through arch near Souris, Manitoba, Canada has no cross bracing between its arches.

The photographer named this abandoned span the "Tick-Swallow" Bridge after discovering that the birds soaring overhead were feeding on a nasty profusion of ticks.

In the tied or "bow string" arch, the lateral thrust is balanced by a tension member connecting the arch ends. This allows for simpler foundations which must resist only vertical forces.

This also allows for very pleasing designs as in the bridge over the Indalsälven River at Stugun, Sweden.

The bow string bridge at Kasba Tadla in Morocco, like the Swedish bridge above, has cross bracing members connecting its arches. This is a more common configuration than on the opposite page.

When an old bridge has become inadequate to meet the demands of modern traffic, a decision must be made whether to enlarge, demolish or supplant the historic span. An important issue in bridge aesthetics ensues when the answer is to build a companion structure.

Tempe, Arizona dealt with this issue with the Mill Avenue Bridge.

1931

1993

Mill Avenue Bridge of 1931 is an open-spandrel concrete deck arch bridge with "Art Deco" touches typical of its age.

When in 1993 traffic volume required a new bridge, the designers of the parallel bridge showed admirable sensitivity to the style of the old span without attempting to duplicate it.

When traffic pressure created the need for this new span at the Crooked River Gorge, the Oregon Department of Transportation realized the importance of designing a bridge which would complement the two historic steel deck arches at the spectacular site. (See page 82.)

Their choice was this clean-lined concrete deck arch with a span of 410 feet.

The new arch is composed of 17 hollow box concrete sections which were poured in place, supported during construction by steel cables attached to 130-foot-high temporary towers.

This picture shows the pour in progress on the final section of the arch.

Concrete Arch Bridges     103

The highway that follows the Pacific Coast of California through the Big Sur crosses a series of deep canyons which are bridged by open-spandrel concrete arches. The most famous and most elegant of these is the Bixby Creek Bridge. The deck is 260 feet above the stream below and the arch spans a distance of 360 feet. The bridge was completed in 1932.

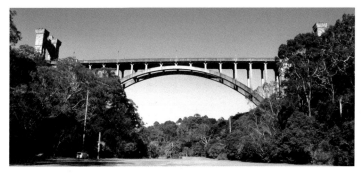

These two bridges have little in common except that both are very uncommon. Northbridge in Sydney, Australia started life in 1892 as a suspension bridge with the distinction of having Australia's longest span until it was surpassed by the Sydney Harbor Bridge in 1932. Then in 1937 it was replaced by this concrete arch but it retained the marvelously ornate stone towers of the old suspension bridge.

The MAX Main Street Bridge in Hillsboro, Oregon was built in 1997 to carry light rail lines over a busy roadway intersection. The bridge is technically a post-tensioned box girder with an arch-supported center pier. The ends of the 110-foot-wide, reinforced concrete arch are linked underground with a post-tensioned tie beam. It is, in other words, a tied arch.

With the development of reinforcing, prestressing and post tensioning, the tensile stength of steel was combined with the compressive strength of concrete, allowing engineers to create new forms and achieve much longer spans in concrete arches. The bridges that follow are examples of some of the most interesting of the long spans that have been realized.

The Paul Sauer or Storms River Bridge in South Africa, built in 1955, was designed by Italian engineer Ricardo Morandi. The arch, which spans 328 feet, was constructed in a unique fashion. The halves of the arch were built with climbing formworks in essentially vertical position on opposite sides of the river canyon and then rotated and lowered into position to form the completed structure.

Redmon Memorial Bridge at Selah Creek in Washington State is actually a matched pair of bridges. One carries northbound and one carries southbound interstate highway traffic. Built in 1971 the 549-foot span still ranks as one of the longest of North America's concrete arches. A rare but welcome sight for the bridge enthusiast is an elaborate roadside park which commands an excellent view of this impressive scene.

The 808-foot concrete arch at Šibenik was built in 1966. It spans a deep inlet on the Adriatic coast of Croatia. The engineer, Ilija Stojadinovic, later designed the world-record spans at Krk. (See page 113.)

When it was built in 1943, Sweden's Sandöbron was the world's longest concrete arch bridge. The graceful 866-foot span held that record until 1963.

There are a variety of obstacles to obtaining a good bridge photograph, but the two most dreaded are bad weather and scaffolding. On my arrival at the Sandöbron, the skies were black, the rain was pelting down and the approach spans were heavily involved in renovation. Suddenly the skies brightened and the main span, unencumbered by construction activity, was posing perfectly for this picture.

On a bridging trip to Porto, Portugal the fascinating 19th century arches over the Douro River (see page 84) made such an impression that the modern Ponte da Arrábida was almost overlooked. This in spite of the fact that when built its span of 890 feet ranked it as Europe's longest concrete arch bridge. The Arrábida Bridge, built in 1963, was designed by Edgar Cardoso. The famous engineer was also responsible for another of Porto's unique spans, the São João Bridge. (See page 9.)

South Africa's "Garden Route" boasts a series of dramatic spans over the rocky gorges along its southern coast. The Paul Sauer Bridge on page 106 is one of these, and pictured here is the largest of the group, the Bloukrans Bridge. Built in 1983, the arch span is 892 feet.

The Gladesville Bridge over the Parramatta River at Sydney, Australia was built in 1959 through 1964 utilizing an interesting construction technique. The arch is formed of precast hollow units which were hoisted onto the centering in much the same way as precut stones were assembled in Roman bridges. The result is an exceptionally graceful landmark on this beautiful waterway. The Gladesville Bridge's span of 1,000 feet was the world's longest concrete arch when completed.

The Island of Krk is connected to the mainland of Croatia by a pair of monumental concrete arches completed in 1980. The larger of the two, pictured here, has a span of 1,280 feet, the world record until it was surpassed in 1997 by a concrete arch in China. The engineer, Ilija Stojadinovic, was earlier responsible for the design of the beautiful arch at Šibenik. (See page 108.)

# BRIDGE TYPES

## Suspension Bridges

Some have described the catenary curve of a suspension bridge as an inverted arch; most will readily agree that suspension bridges can approach the classic arch in aesthetic appeal. In ancient times suspension bridges which depended upon ropes of vines, bamboo or leather were limited by the strength of those materials. In more recent times, chains of iron and then cables of high-strength steel have expanded the modern bridge's ability to attain greater and greater spans, resulting in bridges that defy the imagination while retaining their innate beauty. The bridges that follow are chosen for their eye appeal and arranged more or less in order of length of span.

This ornate footbridge at the Brahesborg Estate in Denmark has a span of just 75 feet. An iron plaque in the portal arch reads, "MDCCCL." The visit there provided no other information about the bridge, but its interesting cast iron verticals, its iron chains and its verdant setting qualified it for inclusion.

A previous reference was made to the dread of scaffolding interfering with bridge photography. A most extreme case was encountered in the Scottish Highlands at the Oich Suspension Bridge. James Dredge built this stone-towered suspension bridge in 1849. The good news is that the bridge is being thoroughly renovated to preserve this example of the unique suspension system Dredge pioneered. The bad news is that this photographer was totally stymied by the protective shrouding.

On a more successful note, these two Scottish footbridges posed most attractively for our visit. Priorsford Bridge at Peebles (on the left) was built by Robert Inglis in 1905. It has a span of 97 feet.

Scotland's Cambus O'May Bridge (right) was also built in 1905. This suspension footbridge has a span of 170 feet.

These two bridges are alike in age and in span, but there the similarity ends. The Ponte della Catena in the vicinity of Bagni de Lucca, Italy was built in 1860. Its deck is carried by iron chains supported by ornate stone arches. It is now restricted to pedestrian traffic only.

The Wire Bridge in New Portland, Maine was built at about the same time but relies on wire suspension cables and shingle-clad wooden towers. It is carefully maintained and still in use for vehicular traffic on its wooden deck. The Italian bridge boasts a span of 165 feet, and the Wire Bridge, 198 feet.

The rigid deck of a modern suspension bridge hangs from the supporting cables, but in ancient bridges the deck usually rested directly on, or followed the curve of, the supporting ropes or vines. Even now there are bridges, appropriately called "swing bridges" in which the deck follows the curve of the cables. They can provide a very exciting way to cross a stream.

At Solstadström, Sweden, the Solstadströmbron Footbridge has a bouncy span of about 250 feet.

The Souris Swingbridge in Manitoba, Canada stretches 264 feet across the Souris River. It is said to date from 1906, but it was obviously newly renovated when this picture was taken.

This stylish span reaches 336 feet over the Oued Skhirat between Rabat and Casablanca in Morocco. Built during the French occupation of Morocco, it is still in regular use, but a modern highway bridge now carries most of the inter-city traffic. It was not identified when featured in the *Bridge of the Month Quiz* website in 2001. Only twice in four years has a bridge stumped the experts.

At Tarassac in Languedoc, France the Pont Suspendu sur l'Orb soars high above the Orb River where the canoers and kayakers enjoy their popular water sports. The bridge itself is more remarkable for its brilliant coat of paint than for its 342-foot span.

If it hadn't been for the advice of a Paris taxi driver, this fascinating bridge wouldn't have been included here. Most of the literature on Paris bridges ignores the Pont du Port L'Anglais. Construction began in 1913 but World War I delayed completion until 1928. The 407-foot span is supported by a unique system of intersecting sets of suspension cables.

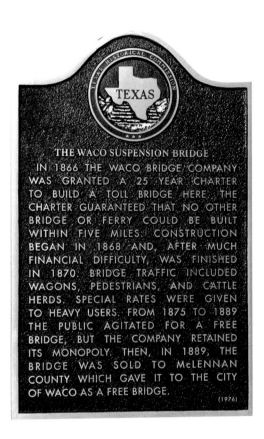

The Waco Suspension Bridge over the Brazos River in Waco, Texas was reputed to be the longest-span suspension bridge west of the Mississippi River when built. The 475-foot span was designed by Thomas M. Griffith to serve wagons, pedestrians and also Texas cattle on its wooden deck. It is now relegated to service as a pedestrian bridge as the well-maintained centerpiece of a city park.

Thomas Telford is sometimes called the father of the modern suspension bridge on the basis of his Menai Straits and Conway bridges in Wales. Both were completed in 1826 in a new road system connecting the Island of Anglesey with the mainland.

The Conway Bridge is blended architecturally with the adjacent Conway Castle (right) and has a span of 380 feet. The Menai Bridge (opposite) was a quantum leap forward with its span of 580 feet. Both bridges are still in use, but only the Menai carries auto traffic.

Six years earlier, in 1820, Captain Samuel Brown built the Union Bridge which crosses the River Tweed to link England with Scotland. The 449-foot span is supported by eyebar suspension chains of his design. It too still carries modern auto traffic, albeit one car at a time.

As the scale of suspension bridges expanded in the mid-19th century, English engineers designed these two monumental bridges that survive today. William Tierney Clark was chosen by Hungarian Count István Széchenyi to build this 666-foot span over the Danube at Budapest. The Széchenyi or Chain Bridge was completed in 1849 and restored after being heavily damaged in World War II.

Isambard Kingdom Brunel was a flamboyant engineer whose accomplishments included many important bridges. In 1831 he won a protracted competition over Telford, Brown and a host of less famous bridge builders for design of the Clifton Suspension Bridge. Construction began in 1836 but due to financial setbacks, completion was delayed until 1864. Brunel died in 1859 and never saw the bridge he fought so hard to create. The 702-foot span still carries traffic 245 feet above the River Avon.

### THE WORLD'S HIGHEST
### SUSPENSION BRIDGE
Royal Gorge, Colorado

Built in 1929 as a tourist attraction, the Royal Gorge Suspension Bridge soars 1,053 feet above the Arkansas River. The span is 880 feet. It still attracts tourists.

### THE WORLD'S LOWEST
### SUSPENSION BRIDGE ?
Quebec, Canada

The Gran'Mère Bridge over the St. Maurice River was built in 1929. Canada's cold winter weather allowed a unique method of construction. The prestressed rope strand cables were laid across the frozen river and then hoisted to the tops of the towers. The 950-foot span is one of many attributed to David B. Steinman.

The first suspension bridge to surpass 1,000 feet in span was Charles Ellet's 1,010-foot Ohio River Bridge at Wheeling, West Virginia. This daring structure was built amid court battles alleging that it was a danger to river navigation. The bridge finally won that fight but lost one to the elements when it was heavily damaged by winds in 1854. Subsequent strengthenings and renovations have enabled it to remain in service into the 21st century.

Ellet's chief rival for suspension bridge opportunities in America was John Roebling. Roebling designed the Ohio River Bridge connecting Cincinnati, Ohio with Covington, Kentucky. The project was commenced in 1857 and completed in 1867, setting a new world record with its span of 1,057 feet. Additional cables and arched trusses have been added over the years to provide the strength to accommodate modern traffic.

New York City affords many opportunities to the bridge enthusiast.  Easily the most famous, of course, is the Brooklyn Bridge with its distinctive gothic stone towers.  Designed by John Roebling and completed in 1883 by his son, Washington Roebling, the span of 1,595 feet was the world record.

Its neighbor, the Manhattan Bridge with its attractive blue steel towers, was completed in 1909.  The span is 1,470 feet.

(The overhead view of the two spans was taken from the World Trade Center towers.)

San Francisco's Golden Gate Bridge gets all of the publicity, but its beauty is rivaled by its neighbor, the San Francisco-Oakland Bay Bridge.  Completed in 1936, the connection between Oakland and San Francisco includes a major cantilever span, a tunnel through Treasure Island and this pair of suspension bridges whose end-to-end 2,310-foot spans share a central anchorage.  Historically, San Francisco Bay is subject to severe earthquakes and in recognition, the cantilever bridge between Treasure Island and Oakland is soon to be replaced by another suspension span.

In 1940 Tacoma, Washington's Narrows Bridge was admired for its slender grace. When four months old, the bridge met a dramatic end, torn apart by aerodynamic forces  The replacement bridge (at left above) was built in 1950 with a wider roadway supported by a deep truss to accommodate those forces. The Askøy Bridge in Norway (at right above) is very similar in size to the original Tacoma Bridge, with a span of 2,789 feet, compared to Tacoma's 2,800, and a narrow two-lane deck.  But that deck is supported by an aerodynamic steel box girder designed to resist the destructive power of the wind. Built in 1993, the Askøy is the longest of the many fine modern suspension bridges in Norway.

Scotland's Forth Road Bridge (left) and Portugal's Ponte 25 de Abril (right) are remarkably similar in many respects. The Queensferry Scotland bridge, which parallels the more famous Firth of Forth Rail Bridge, was completed in 1964 with a span of 3,300 feet. The bridge over the Tagus River at Lisbon was completed two years later with a span of 3,323 feet. Each was for a time Europe's longest span.

The George Washington Bridge over the Hudson River in New York was completed in 1931 with a span of 3,500 feet, almost doubling the prior record. The design by Othmar Ammann originally called for stone cladding on the towers, but for economy the muscular steel towers were left bare - - and impressive.

The Mackinac Bridge in northern Michigan was the crowning achievement of David B. Steinman's distinguished engineering career. The challenges of building a bridge across five miles of the often-treacherous open waters of the Mackinac Straits were considerable. The 3,800-foot main span and two unusually long side spans of 1,800 feet each made it the longest bridge in terms of the total suspended span when it was completed in 1957.

One of my all-time thrills in "bridging" was a guided visit to the top of one of the towers 552 feet above the water.

On the Gulf of Bothnia 300 miles north of Stockholm is an area of islands and inlets called the Höga Kusten or High Coast.

The Höga Kustenbron or High Coast Bridge was completed in 1997 crossing the mouth of the Ångermanälven. The concrete pylons rise 590 feet above the water and are presently the tallest constructions in Sweden. The main span of the bridge is 3,970 feet ranking it first for Swedish bridges and just behind the Golden Gate on the "world's longest" list.

The natural beauty of the site and also the striking red color of the sweeping expanse of the steel box girder remind one of the San Francisco bridge.

The old adage, "a picture is worth a thousand words," is certainly appropriate regarding San Francisco's Golden Gate Bridge. Numerous books have been written about this famous icon, but its beauty speaks for itself. When it was completed in 1937, its 4,200-foot span was the world's longest, and though since surpassed in size, it still can lay claim to the title of "most spectacular."

Othmar Ammann's George Washington Bridge established the world record for length of span in 1931. That figure was surpassed in 1937 by the Golden Gate, but in 1964 Ammann re-took the record with completion of this 4,260-foot span of the Verrazano Narrows Bridge in New York.

China's longest suspension span is the Jiangyin Bridge over the Yangtse River. There is a splendid viewing pavilion adjacent to the bridge, but it required a two hour wait for the morning fog to lift before even this much of the bridge appeared. The 4,544-foot span was completed in 1999.

The dominance of American bridge builders in the long-span race ended with the completion of the Humber Bridge in 1981. This 4,624-foot span crosses the Humber Estuary on the north-east coast of England. Its slim graceful deck is another aerodynamically designed steel box girder. In a departure from previous practice, the connecting cables by which the deck is hung from the main cables are arranged in an inclined or zig-zag pattern rather than the normal vertical configuration.

Completed in 1998, the Great Belt Fixed Link connects Denmark's Islands of Sjælland and Fyn. The total length of the link is almost 11 miles and it includes a railroad tunnel, a combined rail and road bridge and this suspension bridge, the Storebælt Østbroen. The suspension bridge's main span is 5,328 feet, ranking it second only to Japan's Akashi-Kaiko Bridge.

Ordinarily bridges are eliminated from selection for this book if the photographer's efforts fail to capture the image in a pleasing way. Sometimes conditions conspire to produce sub-par results and yet the bridge is of such importance that, with apologies to the reader, a "bad" picture is better than none. The picture above was taken from so far away that the imposing shape of the Østbroen was almost lost in the distance.

# BRIDGE TYPES

## Cable-Stayed Bridges

able-stayed bridges differ from suspension bridges in that the deck is supported by cables attached directly to a pylon rather than being suspended from a catenary cable. While some examples exist in older bridges, the imaginative use of the cable-stay form has been primarily a development of the last half-century. Sizes range from interesting pedestrian bridges to massive structures which approach 3,000 feet in span. The possibilities for interesting variation in the form of the pylons and the arrangement of the cables provide modern bridge designers new opportunities to produce aesthetically pleasing spans.

A worldwide selection of examples starts with Scripps Crossing, a pedestrian overpass on the campus of the Scripps Institution of Oceanography in La Jolla, California. This stunning cable-stayed bridge was built in 1990.

After World War II there was an urgent need to replace the bridges on the Rhine and elsewhere in Europe. German engineers recognized that cable-stay bridges were economical in their use of scarce material and well-suited for major crossings.

The single pylon Severinsbrücke at Cologne which was built in 1959 with a span of 990 feet was one of the early efforts.

The striking single pylon of the Fleherbrücke at Düsseldorf reaches across the Rhine with a span of 1,207 feet. The bridge was completed in 1979.

The Nordhordland Bridge north of Bergen, Norway is an unusual combination of cable-stay and floating bridges. The curving portion in the left of this picture is part of an 4,088-foot pontoon bridge. The cable-stay portion lifts the roadway over the ship channel with a span of 564 feet. The structure was completed in 1994.

Also dating from 1994, the Great River Bridge at Burlington, Iowa crosses the Mississippi River with a cable-stayed span of 660 feet supported by a single pylon. The pier in the foreground, which appears to be a support, is a remnant of the 1917 cantilever bridge and is not connected to the new structure. The derrick in the background is involved in retrofitting the bridge to eliminate disturbing cable vibration.

Built in 1968, Tasmania's Batman Bridge is an early example of an inclined pylon. The A-frame tower leans out over the Tamar River at an angle 20° from vertical to support the 706-foot span. The bridge is not named for the comic book hero, Bat Man, but rather for John Batman, a famous pioneer of Tasmania who also founded the city of Melbourne.

Ordinarily it would be hazardous to stand in the middle of a highway for this view, but this was not a very busy bridge.

At Rotterdam in The Netherlands, the goal was to create a bridge which would connect the city center with the dock area. Moreover, the charge to architect Ben van Berkel was to create a new symbol of the city of Rotterdam in the form of a monumental span. The answer was completed in 1996. The Erasmus Bridge is a single-pylon, asymmetrical, cable-stayed bridge. Its modest suspended span of 932 feet doesn't rank with the major cable-stayed bridges of the world, but its visual impact is unrivaled.

The Willems Bridge shares the same waterway with Rotterdam's more famous Erasmus Bridge (page 145). This interesting cable-stayed bridge was built five years earlier in 1981 and has a main span of 853 feet.

The cable pattern is unique in that the plane is horizontal through the two supporting pylons and twists to vertical alignment where attached to the deck. A book on bridge aesthetics uses this as an example of disorder, but I found the effect visually pleasing.

The Puente Zarate-Brazo Largo crosses the Paraná River just upstream from its confluence with Rio de la Plata in Argentina. Built in 1977, its main span of 1,082 feet towers above the lion colored waters.

Those waters were the play-ground for a group of young daredevils who were intent on showing off for the bridge photographer.

Unlike Australia's Gladesville Bridge (page 112) and the Harbour Bridge (page 93) which both enjoy charming waterfront sites, this handsome bridge crosses Johnston's Bay and a much less charming industrial area of Sydney. The bridge was completed in 1995, replacing the old Glebe Island Bridge and initially adopting that name. In 1998 the bridge was dedicated to the memory of the soldiers of Australia and New Zealand who served in World War I and was officially renamed the Anzac Bridge. The cable-stayed main span is the longest in Australia, 1,132 feet.

Riyadh, Saudi Arabia abounds with interesting modern architecture, but seems an unlikely place to find a cable-stayed bridge with a 1,329-foot main span. The Wadi Laban Bridge was completed in the year 2,000. The gleaming beauty carries six lanes of highway traffic high above this dry river bed on the outskirts of the Saudi capital city.

The Uddevallabron (above left and at right) carries motorway traffic over the Sunnige Sound on Sweden's west coast. The bridge was completed in 2000. It is not very big by modern standards, with a span of 1,358 feet, but the motorist's view through the cathedral-like webs of the towers and cables is in a class by itself.

British Columbia, Canada's Alex Fraser Bridge (below left) reigned as the longest of the world's cable-stay bridges from its completion in 1986 until its 1,526 foot span was surpassed in 1991. Now with the proliferation of major spans around the world, this bridge doesn't even rank in the top 20.

Completed in 2,000, the Öresund Fixed Link which connects Sweden and Denmark consists of a 2+ mile tunnel, a 2+ mile artificial island and a bridge of almost 5 miles. The link provides for a four-lane motorway and a dual-track electrified railway.

The center or High Bridge section is a cable-stayed giant with 670-foot pylons supporting a 1,608-foot main span. The road deck is atop the composite steel and concrete truss girder and the rail tracks are within the girder. The clearance over the waters of the Öresund is 187 feet.

The Skarnsundet Bridge was reached after a long drive north from Trondheim, Norway through a lovely countryside accented by hedgerows of colorful fireweed in full bloom. The show of color was also evident in the surprisingly pink cables supporting the 1,739-foot main span. It is unusual to see such a monumental bridge with only two traffic lanes, but like many of the bridges crossing Norway's fjords, the Skarnsundet is in a remote area with relatively sparse traffic. The bridge was completed in 1993.

Bridging China was a wonderful experience for me and a new experience for my guides. At each city visited it was necessary to convince the local guide that the goal was to see and photograph bridges. Not jade shops, but bridges. Not silk factories, not cloisonné studios, not ceramic workshops, but bridges.

In Shanghai, on our first outing, the guide explained that the driver couldn't stop near the big Nanpu Bridge; consequently the photos would have to be taken on the fly like the picture at left. After I convinced her of the importance of achieving the best vantage point, she was very resourceful. The photos opposite and on the next two pages attest to her efforts.

Shanghai's Nanpu Bridge is the oldest of that city's three modern cable-stay bridges. Built in 1991, it carries six lanes of traffic over the Huangpu River with a span of 1,388 feet.

The Xu Pu Bridge (at left) is another of Shanghai's modern giants. Built in 1997, its span of 1,936 feet over the Huangpu River ranks it 7th on the list of long-span cable-stayed bridges.

In spite of the best efforts of my guide, the Xu Pu Bridge proved elusive, well-concealed at ground level by buildings and trees and without any obvious access to a higher vantage point.

The same seemed to be true at the site of the Yangpu Bridge, but the guide found a way to the upper floors of an almost-completed office tower. The view was ideal except that it was impeded by a very dirty window. In despair I rubbed the glass and was delighted to find that all the dirt was on the inside and easily cleaned to make this shot possible.

The Yangpu Bridge, at right, is the longest of the three Shanghai bridges. Built in 1993, its 1,975-foot span currently ranks it 6th on the list of long-span cable-stayed bridges.

# BRIDGE TYPES

## Moving Bridges

**E**ach of the previous sections has concentrated on aesthetically pleasing spans. When presenting moving bridges the emphasis is necessarily on the "interesting" rather than the beautiful.

The natural conflict between the free flow of waterborne commerce and the bridging of waterways can be resolved in a number of ways. When it is not practical to elevate the bridge sufficiently to avoid obstruction of water traffic, the solution is to construct a bridge which can move out of the way. The common forms of moving bridges are the bascule, the swing bridge and the lift bridge.

A most picturesque version of the bascule bridge is the Pont de Langlois, the subject of a famous painting by Vincent Van Gogh. Built around 1820, it was moved from its original site to this location near Arles, France where it is now maintained as a tourist attraction.

The Skansen Bru at Trondheim, Sweden demonstrates the bascule principal. The counterbalanced deck pivots upward to allow boats to pass this rail bridge. The Skansen is a "single leaf" bascule. The bridge below is a "double leaf" bascule with a counterbalance at each end of the split deck. It is the Isleton Bridge over the Sacramento River in California, built in 1923.

The second type of moving bridge is the swing bridge. In this example, at Newcastle-upon-Tyne, England the bridge rotates on its center to create a ship channel with unobstructed vertical clearance, albeit with considerable obstruction of the center of the River Tyne. This ornate bridge was built in 1876. Robert Stephenson's High Bridge from 1849 dominates the background.

McComb's Dam Bridge is the oldest of the remaining swing bridges over New York City's Harlem River. Built in 1895, it was designed by Alfred P. Boller who was noted for his "artistic" touches.

The pedestrian swing bridge pictured below is at the tourist-oriented Victoria and Alfred Harbour in Capetown, South Africa. Instead of rotating on a central support, this bridge swings like a gate from one end. This is not only a swing bridge, but also a cable-stayed bridge with a span of 105 feet.

The third type of moving bridge is the vertical lift bridge. The movable span is lifted on supporting towers to provide clearance for water traffic.

The Buzzard's Bay Bridge in Massachusetts was built in 1934 and its 550-foot span ranks it as one of the world's longest vertical lift bridges.

At right is the Columbia River Bridge at Wishram, Washington, a typical railroad vertical lift bridge.

The Steel Bridge in Portland, Oregon is the only bridge in the world whose lower (railroad) deck operates independently of the upper road deck. This allows most river traffic to pass under the lifted rail deck without interruption of vehicular traffic. The bridge was built in 1912 and still carries trains, light rail, buses, trucks, autos, bicycles and pedestrians over the Willamette River.

Another very unusual lift bridge is this concrete arch railroad bridge in Stockholm, Sweden. It is actually an approach section of the Årstabron, a steel arch rail bridge built in 1929. (The steel arch bridge is illustrated on page 78.)

A relic from the past and certainly the rarest form of moving bridges is the transporter, transbordeur or transborador. This type carried cross-harbor traffic in gondolas suspended from an overhead superstructure, enabling pedestrian and vehicular traffic to cross busy harbors full of tall ships without obstructing seagoing commerce. While this was effective for a time, the explosive growth of auto traffic soon rendered the form impractical.

French engineer Ferdinand Arnodin was the leading advocate of the transbordeur bridge at the end of the 19th century. He designed, among others, the Newport Transporter Bridge in Wales which was completed in 1906.

This carefully-restored bridge still carries the curious comfortably across the 645-foot span of the muddy River Usk.

A rare pair! Two transborador bridges side by side in Buenos Aires, Argentina. The Transborador del Riachuelo Nicolas Avellaneda (in the foreground) was inaugurated on May 31, 1914. Its gondola (at left) is waiting in vain on the opposite shore -- no longer in use.

The newer bridge in the background is an unusual combination of a vertical lift span and a more modern transborador, both of which are still in use. The third bridge in the distance is the character-less modern motorway span.

# PERSONAL FAVORITES

**A**s much as I try to be fair in the presentation of bridges of all forms, it is probably inevitable that my personal favorites get special attention. The remaining pages are therefore devoted to two personal favorite categories of bridges which have so far been bypassed in the discussion of bridge types.

# AQUEDUCTS

Aqueducts are structures which carry water by gravity from its source to the user. For most of its journey, the path of an aqueduct lies at or below ground level. But where it is necessary to cross a stream or valley, the aqueduct is elevated, sometimes very dramatically elevated, on an aqueduct bridge. Ancient aqueducts are among the most fascinating of the world's bridges.

Typically, the great stone aqueducts of the world are relics of the distant past. But this one is said to date from about 1960. It is in Hebei Province, China near Tianjin City and its very descriptive name is "Aqueduct to make the region flourish."

Most aqueducts are engineered with a very gradual rate of fall, but the Ponte-Acquedotto dei Biscari in the vicinity of Adrano on the island of Sicily is an unusual type, a syphon aqueduct. The channel drops steeply down one side of the valley and ascends on the other. It was built in 1761 to 1791. Originally the water channel was carried over the valley on 31 masonry arches. A modern concrete arch now spans the river itself.

L'acquedotto de Pontecchio near Montalto de Castro in Italy is very reminiscent of the old Roman aqueducts, but it is said to date from the 1700s. The upper arcade was heavily damaged in a wind storm in 1994.

This colonnade of 300 arches is the Aqueduto de Pegões which was built in 1614 to provide water to the Convento de Cristo in the hills above Tomar, Portugal.

There are numerous medieval aqueducts in Portugal but none more accessible or rewarding to the photographer.

The Ponte della Torre in Spoleto, Italy is my favorite of all medieval aqueducts. It is said to have been preceded at this site by an aqueduct from Roman times. The current version dates from the 14th century.

The eleven arches carry not only a water channel but also a footpath 266 feet above the valley floor.

The amazing engineering skills of the Romans are evident in the widespread remains of their mighty aqueducts.

The Aqua Alexandrina is one of eleven aqueducts which served the ancient city of Rome. Built in the 3rd century A.D., the entire structure was 22 km. long, but only a few of its 2 km. of arched arcades remain intact.

The Valens Aqueduct in Istanbul, Turkey was built during the reign of Emperor Hadrian (117 - 138 A.D.) and rebuilt in the time of Emperor Valens (364 - 378 A.D.)

The Los Milagros
aqueduct was one of
three which served
the Roman city at
Mérida, Spain. All
three date from the
Hadrian's time.

The Cornelio Aqueduct
dates from the 2nd century
A.D. The remains of at
least three arcades are
preserved in the hills
above the Sicilian town
of Termini Imerese.

Roman engineering of an impressive scale spread throughout the Empire. Spain and France boast two of the most spectacular of the remaining Roman aqueducts.

The Aqueducto de Segovia dominates the city of Segovia, Spain. The double tier of arches towers 93 feet above street level. The entire bridge portion of the aqueduct consists of 199 spans for a total length of 2,388 feet. Its carefully fitted arch stones were assembled without mortar and have stood since the structure was built in the 1st century A.D.

The Pont du Gard is probably the most famous of all the world's aqueducts. It is the largest elevated section of the conduit built in 18 B.C. to bring water 31 miles to the Roman city of Nemausus, (now known as Nîmes, France). The three tiers tower 160 feet above the River Gard making it the tallest of all Roman bridges. The central arch has a span of 80 feet. The first tier of arches supports a road bridge which was tacked on in the 18th century.

In contrast to Segovia's urban site, the Pont du Gard occupies a charming park-like setting, obviously popular for recreation as well as historical sight seeing.

# PERSONAL FAVORITES

# SPECIAL BRIDGES

he remainder of the bridges in the personal favorites category are titled, for lack of a better term, special bridges. "Special" includes one-of-a-kind bridges; the elegant spans of Santiago Calatrava; and finally, three personal favorites from my own back yard.

Certainly qualifying as a one-of-a-kind, the Bailey Island or Cribstone Bridge in Maine connects that island to the mainland. Its open cribbing of granite slabs allows the strong local tidal flow to pass through the 1,120-foot-long causeway. This unique span was built in 1928.

The Willow Bridge on the Long Dyke at Beijing, China's Summer Palace is one of a number of pavilion-topped stone bridges in the 18th century Imperial Garden. It could be included with the masonry arch bridges or with the beam bridges as its approach spans are arches of stone and its open pavilion sits atop stone slabs. But this beauty clearly belongs to the one-of-a-kind category -- a really special bridge.

The Puente Uriburu in Buenos Aires, Argentina is an ugly steel lift bridge which crosses the polluted channel of the Riachuelo River in a less-than-savory neighborhood in that fascinating city. But at each end of the bridge, the portals are amazingly elegant and quite well maintained, easily qualifying this span for its inclusion in the one-of-a-kind grouping. The bridge which was built in 1938 bears the full name, "PUENTE PRESIDENTE The GENERAL JOSE FELIX URIBURU."

Comácchio is a charming town among Italy's northern Adriatic lagoons. With many small bridges connecting its thirteen islands, it is often called "Little Venice." The most famous and most unusual of the bridges is the Trepponti which is located in the town's center at the confluence of five canals. Built in 1634 by Luca Danesi, this unique structure has long served as a symbol of the city and a delight to tourists.

The Sacramento River Trail Bridge is a concrete stressed ribbon bridge. It was the first of its kind in North America when inaugurated in 1990. The 13-foot-wide, 418-foot-long span contains 236 steel cables inside the bridge deck. The cables are connected to anchors drilled deep into solid bedrock. The bridge is part of a popular recreational trail which follows the Sacramento River in Redding, California.

My research prepared me for the pleasure of visiting the picturesque Puente Sobre el Arroyo Maldonado at La Barra in Uruguay, but not for the surprise of finding two identical bridges at the site.

The first of these two stressed ribbon bridges was built in 1963 to the design of engineer Leonel Viera. The second span (above) was added in 1999. It is not uncommon that growing traffic demands require new bridges alongside old ones, but only rarely is the addition done so tastefully.

The pleasing curvature of the Puente Sobre el Arroyo Maldonado inspired Chilean Nobel Laureate Pablo Neruda to poetry. And it also inspires fun-loving drivers to attempt ill-advised thrill rides.

With the exception of three beam bridges on pages 5 and 6, the wooden bridge has been left out of this presentation. Though the common covered bridge fails to interest me, there are some fascinating one-of-a-kind bridges of wood. The "Mathematical" Bridge at Queens' College in Cambridge, England is one of the most celebrated of the world's wooden spans. The name derives from legend that it was built in 1749 on geometric principles and assembled without nails.

The Keystone Wye Bridge is a laminated wood three-level highway interchange near Rapid City, South Dakota. Completed in 1968, it is one of a kind in my collection and is possibly unique in the world. The designers, Clyde Jundt and Ken Wilson, were charged with providing a wooden structure which would enhance rather than detract from the beauty of its setting. They succeeded.

Trondheim, the original capitol of Norway, is noted for its many charming wooden structures. Prominent among these is another one-of-a-kind wooden bridge. The Old Town Bridge over the River Nid is a simple wooden truss which formerly had a lift section. The movable span is no longer operative. The picturesque portals which supported the lift mechanism are retained, providing the city a colorful landmark known locally as "Lykkens Portal" (The Gate to Happiness).

The most modern of these very distinctive wooden bridges was completed in 2001, but was based on a design from five centuries earlier. Leonardo da Vinci proposed a sweeping stone arch to cross the Golden Horn at Istanbul. That bridge was never built, but the design lived on and was finally realized in this wooden pedestrian arch over a highway intersection in Ås, Norway.

Santiago Calatrava is a Spanish-born architect and engineer whose imaginative creations have set exciting new standards in bridge aesthetics. His imaginative work has also created an outpouring of analysis by doting authors who try to outdo each other in their descriptions of his work. (I have five such volumes in my bridge book collection and could easily have more.) A picture is worth a thousand words.

Puente Lusitania,
Mérida, Spain, 1991

The elegant arch at the left is
the first Calatrava bridge that
I encountered.  It features a
cathedral-like walkway above
the traffic lanes affording an
unobstructed view over the
Guadiana River beside the
ancient Puente Romano.  (See
page 19.)

Puente de Alamillo, Seville, Spain, 1992

Built in conjunction with Seville's Expo in 1992, this bridge has attracted perhaps the most attention and controversy of any of Calatrava's works. The inclined pylon is a steel tower filled with concrete which supports the 656-foot deck.

Puente de la Mujer,  Buenos Aires, Argentina,
2001

At Puerto Madero the old docks have been converted
into an up-scale business and entertainment district.
This cable-stayed Calatrava footbridge over the harbor
rotates on the central pier to allow passage of water
traffic.

Bridging the world requires a lot of traveling and travel is a wonderful thing, but coming home is often the best part of every trip. Coming home to the bridges of my home state, Oregon, is always rewarding. The final section of *Bridging the World* is reserved for three personal favorites from my own back yard.

The Bridge of the Gods which connects Oregon and Washington across the Columbia River is selected for three reasons. First, it has a most appealing name, related to a legendary natural bridge at the same site. Second, it is an excellent example of a cantilever bridge. Third, there is a gift shop located at the Oregon end of the bridge which has consistently sold my bridge books.

The bridges of Conde B. McCullough, some of which are featured on pages 82, 87, 98 and 99, are the most famous Oregon spans and certainly among my personal favorites.   The Alsea Bay Bridge of 1991, pictured here, replaces McCullough's bridge of 1936 at Waldport, Oregon. (See page 98.)  As the removal of the old span was a great disappointment to many of the locals, the new bridge was designed with special concern for its aesthetic appeal.  The gratifying result was this steel tied arch with the approach spans supported on attracive Y-shaped concrete piers.

Portland, Oregon is bisected by the Willamette River and has an abundance of interesting bridges. The only one of these which can truly be called beautiful is the St. Johns Bridge. Its designer David B. Steinman wrote, "In the St. Johns bridge, the desire to secure a beautiful public structure was a governing consideration." The 1,207-foot span made this the longest suspension bridge west of Detroit when it was completed in 1931.

The man standing by the stylized anchorage structure of the St. Johns Bridge is dwarfed by its massive size. Over the years, many critics have labeled the bridge's ornamentation inappropriate. In my opinion, the distinctive towers and the soaring, cathedral-like approach piers make this unique bridge a thing of unusual beauty and a rewarding homecoming view after *Bridging the World*.

# A

# B

# C

# D

# E

# F

# G